The Dodd-Frank Wall Street Reform and Consumer Protection Act: Title VII, Derivatives

Rena S. Miller
Analyst in Financial Economics

Kathleen Ann Ruane
Legislative Attorney

November 6, 2012

Congressional Research Service

7-5700

www.crs.gov

R41398

Summary

The financial crisis implicated the over-the-counter (OTC) derivatives market as a major source of systemic risk. A number of firms used derivatives to construct highly leveraged speculative positions, which generated enormous losses that threatened to bankrupt not only the firms themselves but also their creditors and trading partners. Hundreds of billions of dollars in government credit were needed to prevent such losses from cascading throughout the system. AIG was the best-known example, but by no means the only one.

Equally troublesome was the fact that the OTC market depended on the financial stability of a dozen or so major dealers. Failure of a dealer would have resulted in the nullification of trillions of dollars worth of contracts and would have exposed derivatives counterparties to sudden risk and loss, exacerbating the cycle of deleveraging and withholding of credit that characterized the crisis. During the crisis, all the major dealers came under stress, and even though derivatives dealing was not generally the direct source of financial weakness, a collapse of the $600 trillion OTC derivatives market was imminent absent federal intervention. The first group of Troubled Asset Relief Program (TARP) recipients included nearly all the large derivatives dealers.

The Dodd-Frank Act (P.L. 111-203) sought to remake the OTC market in the image of the regulated futures exchanges. Crucial reforms include a requirement that swap contracts be cleared through a central counterparty regulated by one or more federal agencies. Clearinghouses require traders to put down cash (called initial margin) at the time they open a contract to cover potential losses, and require subsequent deposits (called maintenance margin) to cover actual losses to the position. The intended effect of margin requirements is to eliminate the possibility that any firm can build up an uncapitalized exposure so large that default would have systemic consequences (again, the AIG situation). The size of a cleared position is limited by the firm's ability to post capital to cover its losses. That capital protects its trading partners and the system as a whole.

Swap dealers and major swap participants—firms with substantial derivatives positions—will be subject to margin and capital requirements above and beyond what the clearinghouses mandate. Swaps that are cleared will also be subject to trading on an exchange, or an exchange-like "swap execution facility," regulated by either the Commodity Futures Trading Commission (CFTC) or the Securities and Exchange Commission (SEC), in the case of security-based swaps. All trades will be reported to data repositories, so that regulators will have complete information about all derivatives positions. Data on swap prices and trading volumes will be made public.

The Dodd-Frank Act provides exceptions to the clearing and trading requirements for commercial end-users, or firms that use derivatives to hedge the risks of their nonfinancial business operations. Regulators may also provide exemptions for smaller financial institutions. Even trades that are exempt from the clearing and exchange-trading requirements, however, will have to be reported to data repositories or directly to regulators.

This report describes some of the requirements placed on the derivatives market by the Dodd-Frank Act. It will be updated as events warrant.

Contents

Figures

Contacts

Introduction

Prior to the financial crisis that began in 2007, over-the-counter (OTC) derivatives were generally regarded as a beneficial financial innovation that distributed financial risk more efficiently and made the financial system more stable, resilient, and resistant to shocks. The crisis essentially reversed this view. The Dodd-Frank Act (P.L. 111-203) attempts to address the aspect of the OTC market that appeared most troublesome in the crisis: the market permitted enormous exposure to risk to grow out of the sight of regulators and other traders. Derivatives exposures that could not be readily quantified exacerbated panic and uncertainty about the true financial condition of other market participants, contributing to the freezing of credit markets. Under Dodd-Frank, risk exposures of major financial institutions must be backed by capital, minimizing the shock to the financial system should such a firm fail. In addition, regulators will have information about the size and distribution of possible losses during periods of market volatility.

Background

Derivative contracts are an array of financial instruments with one feature in common: their value is linked to changes in some underlying variable, such as the price of a physical commodity, a stock index, or an interest rate. Derivatives contracts—futures contracts, options, and swaps[1]— gain or lose value as the underlying rates or prices change, even though the holder may not actually own the underlying asset.

Thousands of firms use derivatives to manage risk. For example, a firm can protect itself against increases in the price of a commodity that it uses in production by entering into a derivative contract that will gain value if the price of the commodity rises. A notable instance of this type of hedging strategy was Southwest Airlines' derivatives position that allowed it to buy jet fuel at a low fixed price in 2008 when energy prices reached record highs. When used to hedge risk, derivatives can protect businesses (and sometimes their customers as well) from unfavorable price shocks.

Others use derivatives to seek profits by betting on which way prices will move. Such speculators provide liquidity to the market—they assume the risks that hedgers wish to avoid. The combined trading activity of hedgers and speculators provides another public benefit: price discovery. By incorporating all known information and expectations about future prices, derivatives markets generate prices that often serve as a reference point for transactions in the underlying cash markets.

Although derivatives trading had its origins in agriculture, today most derivatives are linked to financial variables, such as interest rates, foreign exchange, stock prices and indices, and the creditworthiness of issuers of bonds. The market is measured in the hundreds of trillions of dollars, and billions of contracts are traded annually.

Derivatives have also played a part in the development of complex financial instruments, such as bonds backed by pools of other assets. They can be used to create "synthetic" securities—

---

[1] For a description of the mechanics of these contracts, see CRS Report R40646, *Derivatives Regulation and Legislation Through the 111th Congress*, by Rena S. Miller.

contracts structured to replicate the returns on individual securities or portfolios of stocks, bonds, or other derivatives. Although the basic concepts of derivative finance are neither new nor particularly difficult, much of the most sophisticated financial engineering of the past few decades has involved the construction of increasingly complex mathematical models of how markets move and how different financial variables interact. Derivatives trading is often a primary path through which such research reaches the marketplace.

Since 2000, growth in derivatives markets has been explosive (although the financial crisis has caused some retrenchment since 2008). Between 2000 and the end of 2008, the volume of derivatives contracts traded on exchanges,[2] such as futures exchanges, and the notional value of total contracts traded in the over-the-counter (OTC) market[3] grew by 475% and 522%, respectively. By contrast, during the credit and housing booms that occurred over the same period, the value of corporate bonds and home mortgage debt outstanding grew by only 95% and 115%, respectively.[4] Following the 2008 financial crisis, the total notional value of OTC derivatives globally fell about 13%, but then crept upward again.[5] Total notional values outstanding for OTC derivatives globally fell from $684 trillion as of June 2008, to $592 trillion in December 2008, and then rose again to $648 trillion as of December, 2011.[6]

Pre-Dodd-Frank Act Market Structure and Regulation

The various types of derivatives are used for the same purposes—avoiding business risk, or hedging, and taking on risk in search of speculative profits. Prior to the Dodd-Frank Act, however, the instruments were traded on different types of markets. Futures contracts are traded on exchanges regulated by the Commodity Futures Trading Commission (CFTC); stock options on exchanges under the Securities and Exchange Commission (SEC); and all swaps (and security-based swaps, as well as some options) were traded over-the-counter, and were not regulated by anyone.

Exchanges are centralized markets where all the buying and selling interest comes together. Traders who want to buy (or take a long position) interact with those who want to sell (or go short), and deals are made and prices reported throughout the day. In the OTC market, contracts are made bilaterally, typically between a dealer and an end user, and there was generally no requirement that the price, the terms, or even the existence of the contract be disclosed to a regulator or to the public.

---

[2] See Bank for International Settlements (BIS), Table 23B, for year 2000 turnover for derivative financial instruments traded on organized exchanges, available at http://www.bis.org/publ/qtrpdf/r_qa0206.pdf. For December 2008 figures for derivatives traded on organized exchanges, see BIS Quarterly Review, September 2009, International Banking and Financial Market Developments, available at http://www.bis.org/publ/qtrpdf/r_qt0909.pdf.

[3] See Bank for International Settlements (BIS), Statistical Annex, Table 19, December, 2000 figure for notional amount of total OTC contracts, available at http://www.bis.org/publ/qtrpdf/r_qa0206.pdf. See Bank for International Settlements (BIS), BIS Quarterly Review, September 2009, Statistical Annex, Table 19, for December 2008 figure for notional amount of total OTC contracts, available at http://www.bis.org/publ/qtrpdf/r_qa0909.pdf.

[4] Federal Reserve, *Flow of Funds Accounts of the United States*, September 17, 2009, accessible at http://www.federalreserve.gov/releases/z1/Current/z1r-1.pdf.

[5] See Bank for International Settlements, "Statistical Release: OTC Derivatives Statistics at end-December 2011," published May, 2012. For additional details on OTC derivatives market trends over time, please see their chart on page 2. Available at http://www.bis.org/publ/otc_hy1205.pdf.

[6] Ibid.

Derivatives can be volatile contracts, and the normal expectation is that there will be big gains and losses among traders. As a result, there is an issue of market integrity. How do the longs know that the shorts will be able to meet their obligations, and vice versa? A market where billions of contracts change hands is impossible if all traders must investigate the creditworthiness of the other trader, or counterparty. The exchange market deals with this credit risk problem in one way, the OTC market in another way. How this risk—often called counterparty risk—must be managed was a key element of the reforms implemented by the Dodd-Frank Act.

Market Structure for Cleared and Exchange-Traded Derivatives

The exchanges deal with the issue of credit risk with a clearinghouse.[7] The process is shown in **Figure 1** below. (1) Two traders agree on a transaction on the exchange floor or on an electronic platform. (2) Once the trade is made, it goes to the clearinghouse, which guarantees payment to both parties. (3) In effect, the original contract between long and short traders is now two contracts, one between each trader and the clearinghouse. Traders then do not have to worry about counterparty default because the clearinghouse stands behind all trades.

But the credit risk remains: how does the clearinghouse ensure that it can meet its obligations? Clearing depends on a system of margin, or collateral. Before the trade, both the long and short traders have to deposit an initial margin payment with the clearinghouse to cover potential losses. Then at the end of each trading day, all contracts are repriced, or "marked to market," and all those who have lost money (because prices moved against them) must post additional margin (called variation or maintenance margin) to cover those losses before the next trading session. This is known as a margin call: traders must make good on their losses immediately, or their broker may close out their positions when trading opens the next day. The effect of the margin system is that no one can build up a large paper loss that could damage the clearinghouse in case of default: it is certainly possible to lose large amounts of money trading on the futures exchanges, but only on a "pay as you go" basis.

---

[7] Also referred to as a central counterparty or as a derivatives clearing organization (DCO).

**Figure 1. Pre-Dodd-Frank Act Derivatives Market Structures:
Exchange and Over-the-Counter (OTC)**

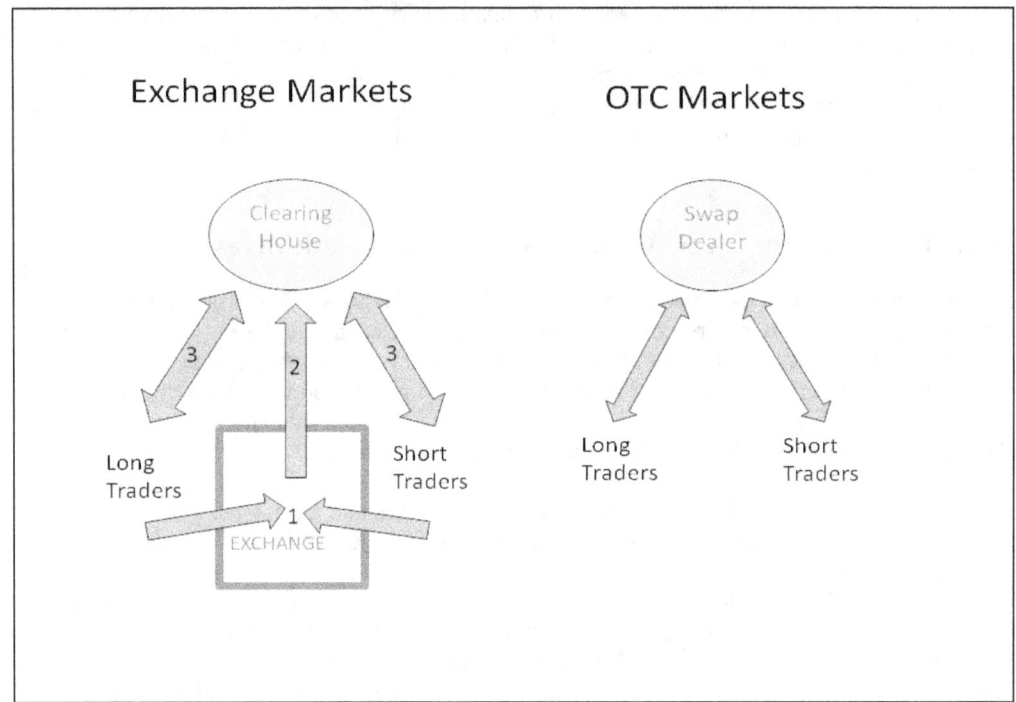

Source: CRS.

Market Structure for OTC Derivatives

In the OTC market, as shown on the right side of **Figure 1**, the long and short traders do not interact directly. Instead of a centralized marketplace, there is a network of dealers who stand ready to take either long or short positions, and make money on spreads and fees. The dealer absorbs the credit risk of customer default, while the customer faces the risk of dealer default. In this kind of market, one would expect the dealers to be the most solid and creditworthy financial institutions, and in fact the OTC market that emerged has been dominated by a dozen or so firms—very large institutions like JP Morgan Chase, Goldman Sachs, Citigroup, Bank of America, Morgan Stanley and their foreign counterparts. Before 2007, such firms were generally viewed as too well diversified or too well managed to fail; in 2008, their fallibility was well established, and a pertinent question now is whether the government would still consider them to be too big to fail. (Title II of Dodd-Frank seeks to ensure that it will not.[8])

In the OTC market, some contracts required collateral or margin, but not all. There was no standard practice: all contract terms were negotiable. A trade group, the International Swaps and Derivatives Association (ISDA), published best practice standards for use of collateral, but compliance was voluntary.

---

[8] See CRS Report R41350, *The Dodd-Frank Wall Street Reform and Consumer Protection Act: Issues and Summary*, coordinated by Baird Webel.

Because there was no universal, mandatory system of margin, large uncollateralized losses could (and did) build up in the OTC market. Perhaps the best-known example in the crisis was AIG, which wrote about $1.8 trillion worth of credit default swaps guaranteeing payment if certain mortgage-backed securities defaulted or experienced other "credit events."[9] Many of AIG's contracts required it to post collateral as the credit quality of the underlying referenced securities (or AIG's own credit rating) deteriorated, but AIG did not post initial margin, as this was deemed unnecessary because of the firm's triple-A rating. As the subprime crisis worsened, AIG faced margin calls that it could not meet. To avert bankruptcy, with the risk of global financial chaos, the Federal Reserve and the Treasury put tens of billions of dollars into AIG, the bulk of which went to its derivatives counterparties.[10]

A key reform in Dodd-Frank is a mandate that many OTC swaps be cleared, which means that they will be subject to margin requirements. This will have the effect of combining features of the two market structures shown in **Figure 1**.

The Dodd-Frank Act's Clearing and Reporting Requirements

The Dodd-Frank Act requires that most derivatives contracts formerly traded exclusively in the OTC market be cleared and traded on exchanges. Traders in these products now are required to post margin in the fashion described above and have their contracts repriced at the close of each trading day. It is important to note that not all derivatives contracts are required to be traded in this way by the act. The Dodd-Frank Act presumes that some derivatives contracts will still be traded in the OTC market; however, it grants regulators broader powers to obtain information about these derivatives and impose margin and capital requirements on them as well. The CFTC and the SEC have been working to issue regulations that implement these provisions.

Clearing Requirement

Title VII of the Dodd-Frank Act creates largely parallel clearing and exchange trading requirements for swaps and security-based swaps as those terms are defined by Title VII and further clarified by the CFTC and the SEC in a joint rulemaking.[11] Section 723 creates the clearing and exchange trading requirements for swaps over which the CFTC has jurisdiction.[12] Section 763 creates largely parallel requirements for security-based swaps over which the SEC has authority.[13]

---

[9] The credit events that trigger credit swap payments may include ratings downgrades, debt restructuring, late payment of interest or principal, as well as default.

[10] For an account of this process, see Office of the Special Inspector General for the Troubled Asset Relief Program ("SIGTARP"), *Factors Affecting Efforts to Limit Payments to AIG Counterparties*, November 17, 2009.

[11] 17 Fed. Reg. 48208, available at http://www.cftc.gov/ucm/groups/public/@lrfederalregister/documents/file/2012-18003a.pdf.

[12] Section 723 of the Dodd-Frank Act (codified at 7 U.S.C. §2).

[13] Section 763(a) of the Dodd-Frank Act (codified at 15 U.S.C. § 78a *et seq.*).

If a swap or security-based swap is required to be cleared, the Dodd-Frank Act makes it unlawful for parties to enter into swaps or security-based swaps unless the transaction has been submitted for clearing.[14] There are two ways in which a swap or security-based swap may become subject to the clearing requirement.[15] In the first way, the agency of jurisdiction is required to engage in an ongoing review of the products it has jurisdiction over to determine whether a particular swap, security-based swap, group, or class of such contracts should be subject to the clearing requirement. Determinations made on the initiative of the commissions are discussed further in the "Prevention of Evasion" section below.

The second way in which a swap or security-based swap may become subject to the clearing requirement under the Dodd-Frank Act is upon submission to the CFTC or the SEC. In the joint rules issued by the CFTC and SEC further defining swaps and security-based swaps, any person may submit a request to the CFTC or the SEC for a public interpretation of whether an instrument is covered by this title.[16] Furthermore, when a derivatives clearing organization[17] (swaps) or clearing agency[18] (security-based swaps) decides to accept a swap or security-based swap for clearing, the act requires the organization to submit the transactions to the relevant commission for a determination as to whether the transactions should be required to be cleared. Furthermore, upon enactment of the Dodd-Frank Act, all swaps and security-based swaps that were listed for clearing by derivatives clearing organizations and clearing agencies at the time of passage were deemed submitted to the SEC and the CFTC for a determination of whether the clearing requirement should apply.

Following submission to the agencies, the agencies have 90 days to determine whether the swaps or security-based swaps are subject to the clearing requirement, unless the submitting organization agrees to an extension. When making that determination, the agencies must consider (1) "the existence of significant outstanding notional exposures, trading liquidity, and adequate pricing data"; (2) "the availability of rule framework, capacity, operational expertise and resources, and credit support infrastructure to clear the contract on terms consistent with material terms and trading conventions on which the contract is then traded"; (3) "the effect on the mitigation of systemic risk ..."; (4) "the effect on competition, including appropriate fees and charges ..."; and (5) "the existence of reasonable legal certainty in the event of the insolvency of the relevant derivatives clearing organization or 1 or more of its clearing members with regard to the treatment of customer and swap counterparty positions, funds, and property."[19] In the process

---

[14] Section 723(a)(3) of the Dodd-Frank Act (codified at 7 U.S.C. §2(h)(1)) (swaps); Section 763(a) of the Dodd-Frank Act (codified at 15 U.S.C. § 78a *et seq.*)(security-based swaps).

[15] Section 723(a)(3) of the Dodd-Frank Act (codified at 7 U.S.C. §2(h)(2)) (swaps); Section 763(a) of the Dodd-Frank Act (codified at 15 U.S.C. § 78a *et seq.*)(security-based swaps).

[16] 17 Fed. Reg. 48208, available at http://www.cftc.gov/ucm/groups/public/@lrfederalregister/documents/file/2012-18003a.pdf.

[17] Rules for the registration and regulation of derivatives clearing organizations are enacted by Section 725 of the Dodd-Frank Act (codified at 7 U.S.C. §7a-1). The CFTC has implemented this section further defining entities that are considered DCOs. 76 Fed. Reg. 69334, available at http://www.cftc.gov/ucm/groups/public/@lrfederalregister/documents/file/2011-27536a.pdf.

[18] Rules for the registration and regulation of clearing agencies were enacted by Section 763(b) of the Dodd-Frank Act (codified at 15 U.S.C. §78a-1). The SEC rulemaking process regarding clearing agency standards is ongoing. The agency has proposed rules to implement registration requirements and other standards, available at http://www.sec.gov/rules/proposed/2011/34-64017.pdf.

[19] Section 723(a)(3) of the Dodd-Frank Act (codified at 7 U.S.C. §2(h)) (swaps); Section 763(a) of the Dodd-Frank Act (codified at 15 U.S.C. § 78a *et seq.*)(security-based swaps). Similar considerations were mandated by the Senate passed version of the bill, but those considerations were to be applied to the agencies' rulemakings to identify other classes of (continued...)

---

of making these determinations, the agencies are also required to allow the public to comment on whether the clearing requirement should apply.

Should the CFTC or the SEC determine that a particular swap or security-based swap is required to be cleared, counterparties to that type of transaction may apply to stay the clearing requirement until the relevant agency "completes a review of the terms" of the swap or security-based swap and the clearing requirement.[20] Under the act, upon completing the review, the relevant agency may require the swap or security-based swap to be cleared, either unconditionally or subject to appropriate conditions. The relevant agency may also determine that the swap or security-based swap is not required to be cleared.

With certain exceptions, for example if one of the counterparties qualifies for the end-user exemption, counterparties to swaps and security-based swaps that are required to be cleared must either execute the transactions on exchanges or specialized execution facilities.[21]

As of this writing, the clearing requirement for swaps has yet to take effect. The CFTC is in the process of implementing the clearing requirement for many derivatives contracts. Rules were proposed in August and the initial comment period closed in September of 2012.[22] The SEC has issued final rules for the mandatory clearing of security-based swaps.[23]

The Exchange-Trading Requirement

With certain exceptions, swaps and security-based swaps that are required to be cleared must also be executed on a regulated exchange or on a trading platform defined in the act as a swaps execution facility (SEF) or a security-based swaps execution facility (SBSEF). Such facilities must permit multiple market participants to trade by accepting bids or offers made by multiple participants in the facility.

The goal of the trading requirement is "to promote pre-trade price transparency in the swaps market."[24] Because the old OTC market was notably opaque, with complete price information available only to dealers, swaps customers were limited in their ability to shop for the best price or rate. The expectation is that as price information becomes more widely available, competition will produce narrower spreads by lowering prices.

(...continued)

transactions that should be subject to the clearing requirement that had not been submitted to the agency. Section 723(a) of H.R. 4173 (as passed by the Senate).

[20] Section 723(a)(3) of the Dodd-Frank Act (codified at 7 U.S.C. §2(h)(3)) (swaps); Section 763(a) of the Dodd-Frank Act (codified at 15 U.S.C. § 78a *et seq.*)(security-based swaps).

[21] Section 723(a)(3) of the Dodd-Frank Act (codified at 7 U.S.C. §2(h)(8)); Section 763(a) of the Dodd-Frank Act (codified at 15 U.S.C. § 78a *et seq.*)(security-based swaps).

[22] 77 Fed. Reg. 47170 (August 7, 2012) available at http://www.cftc.gov/ucm/groups/public/@lrfederalregister/documents/file/2012-18382a.pdf.

[23] SEC, Process for Submissions for Review of Security-Based Swaps for Mandatory Clearing and Notice Filing Requirements for Clearing Agencies; Technical Amendments to Rule 19b-4 and Form 19b-4 Applicable to All Self Regulatory Organizations, Final Rule, Release No. 34-67286 (June 28, 2012) available at http://www.sec.gov/rules/final/2012/34-67286.pdf.

[24] Section 723 of the Dodd-Frank Act (new section 5h(e) of the Commodity Exchange Act to be codified after 7 U.S.C. §7b-2).

SEFs and SBSEFs must comply with a number of core principles set out in the act. While these are somewhat less prescriptive than the regulation of exchanges where public customers are allowed to trade,[25] the new trading facilities have regulatory and administrative responsibilities far beyond what applied to OTC trading desks in the past. Among other things, SEFs and SBSEFs must

- establish and enforce rules to prevent trading abuses and to provide impartial access to the trading facility;

- ensure that swap contracts are not readily susceptible to manipulation;

- monitor trading to prevent manipulation, price distortion, and disruptions in the underlying cash market;

- set position limits;

- maintain adequate financial and managerial resources, including safeguards against operational risk;

- maintain an audit trail of all transactions;

- publish timely data on prices and trading volume;

- adopt emergency rules governing liquidation or transfer of trading positions as well as trading halts; and

- employ a chief compliance officer, who will submit an annual report to regulators.

During consideration of Dodd-Frank, a central issue of debate was the extent to which existing OTC derivatives trading platforms and mechanisms could be accommodated under the new regulatory regime. OTC trading practices ranged from individual telephone negotiations to electronic systems accessible to multiple participants. One concern was that if SEFs were too much like exchanges, the existing futures and securities exchanges would monopolize trading. On the other hand, if the SEF definition were too vague or general, the OTC market might remain opaque.

The bill reported by the Senate Banking Committee defined SEF as "an electronic trading system with pre-trade and post-trade transparency."[26] The explicit reference to "pre-trade" transparency does not appear in the final legislation, in part because of concerns that such a requirement was not compatible with the business models of a number of intermediaries, such as interdealer swap brokers providing anonymous execution services.[27]

As is the case with the clearing requirement, Dodd-Frank provides exceptions to the exchange-trading mandate. If no exchange or SEF or SBSEF makes a swap available for trading, the contract may be traded OTC. A swap that meets the end-user clearing exemption is likewise exempt from the exchange trading requirement. We discuss the end-user exemption in more detail in the next section.

---

[25] Only eligible contract participants will be able to trade on SEFs and SBSEFs.

[26] Section 720 of S. 3217, as reported by the Senate Committee on Banking, Housing, and Urban Affairs, April 15, 2010.

[27] Section 720 of the Dodd-Frank Act, P.L. 111-203.

The CFTC issued a proposed rule, on January 7, 2011, that would further define certain minimum requirements for swap execution facilities.[28] The proposed definition of SEF is parallel to the existing Commodity Exchange Act definition of "trading facility"—a platform where multiple participants have the capacity to post bids and offers to all other parties participating in the facility. The rules would exclude "one-to-one" systems such as telephone voice brokers, and "one-to-many" platforms such as single-dealer trading facilities. Such systems, in the CFTC's view, are not compatible with impartial access requirements of the statute.[29]

SEFs will provide pre-trade price transparency—the ability for all market participants to see quoted prices before transacting—for (1) trades that must be cleared; (2) for all swaps that are made available for trading on a SEF; and (3) trades that are below the size of a block trade. Pre-trade transparency requirements will not apply to (1) block trades, (2) end-user trades, or (3) contracts that are not available for trading on a SEF. Price data will be made public according to the rules on real-time reporting discussed above.

The SEC issued a proposed rule on security-based swap execution facilities on February 2, 2011.[30] The rule appears to be generally similar to the CFTC's SEF proposal. The principal requirement for a security-based SEF is that it be a system or platform that allows more than one participant to interact with the trading interest of more than one other participant on the system or platform.

End-User Exemption

Sections 723 and 763 of the Dodd-Frank Act provide exceptions to the clearing requirement for swaps and security-based swaps when one of the counterparties to the transaction is not a financial entity; is using the transaction to hedge or mitigate its own commercial risk; and notifies the relevant agency "how it generally meets its financial obligations associated with entering into non-cleared swaps."[31] This has been widely referred to as the end-user exemption because it applies only to transactions where at least one counterparty is "not a financial entity."[32]

A financial entity for the purposes of this section is defined as a swap dealer, a security-based swap dealer, a major swap participant (MSP), a major security-based swap participant, a commodity pool, a private fund, an employee benefit plan, or a person predominantly engaged in activities that are in the business of banking, or in activities that are financial in nature.[33] To illustrate, a prime example of an entity that would not be a financial entity, but that may engage in swaps trading as a necessary part of the entity's business, would be an airline that regularly trades

---

[28] Commodity Futures Trading Commission, "Core Principles and Other Requirements for Swap Execution Facilities," Vol. 76 No. 5, *Federal Register* p. 1214, January 7, 2011. And at 17 C.F.R. § 37.

[29] See Commodity Futures Trading Commission, "Core Principles and Other Requirements for Swap Execution Facilities," Vol. 76 No. 5, *Federal Register* p. 1214, January 7, 2011, at p. 1219.

[30] SEC, "Registration and Regulation of Security-Based Swap Execution Facilities," (Release No. 34-63825; File No. S7-06-11), February 2, 2011 available at http://sec.gov/rules/proposed/2011/34-63825.pdf.

[31] Section 723(a)(3) of the Dodd-Frank Act (codified at 7 U.S.C. §2(h)(7)) (swaps); Section 763(a) of the Dodd-Frank Act (codified at 15 U.S.C. § 78a *et seq.*)(security-based swaps).

[32] *Id.*

[33] Section 723(a)(3) of the Dodd-Frank Act (codified at 7 U.S.C. §2(h)(7)) (swaps); Section 763(a) of the Dodd-Frank Act (codified at 15 U.S.C. § 78a *et seq.*)(security-based swaps). (page 822 and 1060).

---

in fuel derivatives to offset potential volatility in the market for jet fuel.[34] Under the act, eligible counterparties may also use an affiliate ("including affiliate entities predominantly engaged in providing financing for the purchase of the merchandise or manufactured goods of the person") to engage in swaps or security-based swaps under the condition that the affiliate "act on behalf of the person [qualifying for the exemption] and as an agent, uses the swap to hedge or mitigate the commercial risk of the person or other affiliate of the person that is not a financial entity."[35] Financial entities wholly controlled by the end-user and whose primary business is hedging the commercial risk of the end user may also qualify for the end-user exemption. Finally, the act allows regulators to exclude depository institutions, farm credit institutions, and credit unions with $10 billion or less in assets from the definition of "financial entity," allowing small financial entities (e.g., small banks) to qualify for the end-user exemption as well.[36]

In order to qualify for the exemption from the clearing requirement, it is not enough to be a non-financial entity (or, in some circumstances a financial entity that qualifies for the exemption, nonetheless). The swaps engaged in by the entity must be for the purpose of hedging or mitigating commercial risk. According to the CFTC's final rule defining the end-user exemption, an entity will be engaging in a swap to hedge or mitigate its own commercial risk under the following circumstances. First, the swap must meet one of the following three criteria. It must be economically appropriate to the reduction of risks conducted by the company; it must qualify as a bona fide hedge for purposes of being exempt from position limits under the CEA; or, it must qualify for hedging treatment under Financial Accounting Standards Board Accounting Standards Codification Topic 815, Derivatives and Hedging (formerly known as Statement No. 133) or Governmental Accounting Standards Board Statement 53, Accounting and Financial Reporting for Derivative Instruments. Second, the swap must not be used either for "a purpose that is in the nature of speculation, investing or trading," or "to hedge or mitigate the risk of another swap or security-based swap position, unless that other position itself is used to hedge or mitigate commercial risk."[37]

The application of the clearing exemption provided by Sections 723 and 763 of the Dodd-Frank Act is at the discretion of the counterparty that qualifies for the exemption. Eligible counterparties may elect to clear the transaction, and may choose which derivatives clearing organization or clearing agency shall clear the transaction. If the eligible counterparty chooses to use the end-user exemption, however, the counterparty must disclose the transaction to the relevant regulator and inform the regulator "how it generally meets its financial obligations associated with entering into

---

[34] Ben Protess, In New Rules to Shine Light on Derivatives, Regulators Also Allow Exemptions, DealBook NYTimes Blog (July 10, 2012), http://dealbook.nytimes.com/2012/07/10/in-new-rules-to-shine-light-on-derivatives-regulators-also-allow-exemptions/.

[35] Affiliates of persons qualifying for the end user exception are not eligible to engage in swaps or security-based swaps on the behalf of qualifying persons if the affiliate is a swap dealer, security-based swap dealer, major swap participant, major security-based swap participant, companies that would be investment companies under section 3 of the Investment Company Act of 1940 but for the exceptions provided in subparagraphs (c)(1) or (c)(7) of that section (15 U.S.C. §80a-3), a commodity pool, or a bank holding company with over $50, 000,000,000 in consolidated assets. Section 723(a)(3) of the Dodd-Frank Act (codified at 7 U.S.C. §2(h)(3)) (swaps); Section 763(a) of the Dodd-Frank Act (codified at 15 U.S.C. § 78a *et seq.*)(security-based swaps).

[36] Section 723(a)(3) of the Dodd-Frank Act (codified at 7 U.S.C. §2(h)(7)) (swaps); Section 763(a) of the Dodd-Frank Act (codified at 15 U.S.C. § 78a *et seq.*)(security-based swaps). The CFTC has also issued rules implementing Section 723, available at http://www.cftc.gov/ucm/groups/public/@newsroom/documents/file/federalregister071012.pdf.

[37] CFTC, End User Exception to the Clearing Requirement for Swaps, RIN 3038-AD10 (September 17, 2012) available at http://www.cftc.gov/ucm/groups/public/@newsroom/documents/file/federalregister071012.pdf.

---

non-cleared swaps."[38] It is also important to note that this exemption applies on a swap by swap basis. As a result, even though a non-financial entity can use the exemption for swaps in which it engages that are related to legitimate hedging activities, if other swaps to which the non-financial entity is a party do not meet the requirements for the definition of a legitimate hedge, laid out by the CFTC, those swaps will be required to be cleared.

The CFTC rules implementing this exemption were issued in September of 2012. However, the rules will not officially apply until the clearing requirement takes effect. As noted above, the CFTC has not yet issued final rules implementing the clearing requirement.

The SEC has proposed rules to implement the end-user exemption for security-based swaps.[39] The rules have yet to become final.

Major Swap Participant and Swap Dealer Definitions

A basic theme in Dodd-Frank is that systemically important financial institutions should maintain capital cushions above and beyond what specific regulations require in order to compensate for the risk that their failure would pose to the financial system and the economy. In addition to the margin requirements that apply to individual derivatives contracts, major participants in derivatives markets will become subject to prudential regulation in Title VII. Two categories of regulated market participants are enumerated: swap dealers and major swap participants (together with the security-based swap equivalents).

Since the OTC dealer market is highly concentrated, the proposal that swap dealers be subject to additional prudential regulation was not controversial. Only a few dozen of the largest financial institutions were presumed to be affected. The question of how many firms should be included in the definition of major swap participant (MSP), however, was contentious. How many non-dealer and non-bank firms should become subject to prudential regulation?

Several MSP definitions were considered in the House; the version of H.R. 4173 that passed the House in December 2009 defined an MSP as a non-dealer holding a "substantial net position" in swaps, excluding positions held to hedge commercial risk, or whose counterparties would suffer "significant credit losses" in the event of an MSP default.[40] Neither "substantial net position," "significant loss," nor "commercial risk" was defined in the bill. However, the bill provided guidance to regulators: the first two terms were linked to "systemically important entities" that can "significantly impact the financial system through counterparty credit risk."

The MSP definition in the bill that passed the House in December 2009 sought to prevent regulators from defining the key terms ("substantial position, "significant loss," etc.) in a way that imposed prudential regulation on most firms that used derivatives to hedge risk. In addition, MSPs were required to clear their swap contracts, and the cost of clearing was regarded as burdensome for end-users. Under the House definition, it seemed plausible that relatively few

---

[38] Section 723(a)(3) of the Dodd-Frank Act (codified at 7 U.S.C. §2(h)(7)) (swaps); Section 763(a) of the Dodd-Frank Act (codified at 15 U.S.C. § 78a *et seq.*)(security-based swaps).

[39] SEC, End-User Exception to the Clearing Requirement for Security-Based Swaps, Docket No. 34-63556 (December 15, 2010) available at http://www.sec.gov/rules/proposed/2010/34-63556.pdf.

[40] Section 3101 of H.R. 4173, as passed the House of Representatives, December 11, 2009.

firms would be defined as MSPs—Fannie Mae and Freddie Mac, a few large non-dealer banks and insurance companies, and perhaps a few large hedge funds.

Figure 2. Global OTC Derivatives Contracts by Type of Counterparty: 2009 and 2011

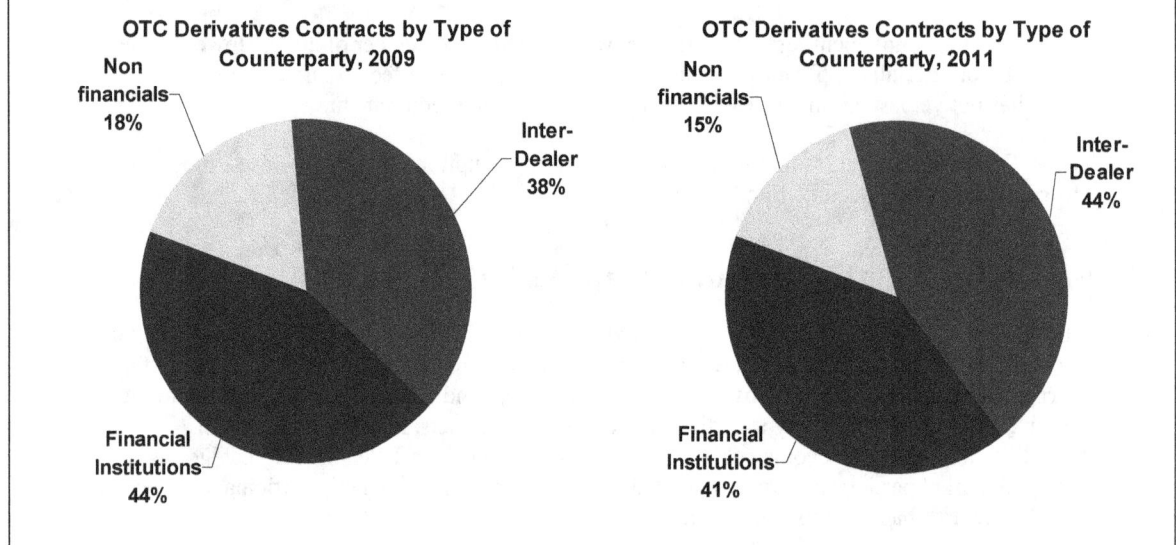

Source: Bank for International Settlements, *Regular OTC Derivatives Market Statistics*, May 2010 and May 2012.

Notes: Includes interest rate, foreign exchange, equity, and credit default swaps. Because this chart describes the global market, which may fall outside United States jurisdiction, some contracts covered by the chart will not be covered by Dodd-Frank regulations.

There was an opposite concern: that if the end-user exemption were too broad, and the MSP definition too narrow, significant volumes of OTC trading might escape the new regulatory scheme. Error! Reference source not found. above suggests that if mandatory clearing were applied only to inter-dealer trades in 2009, nearly two-thirds of the market would be unaffected. Nearly half the OTC contracts in 2009 were between a dealer and another financial institution: how many of these would be covered? While only 18% of transactions in 2009 involved nonfinancial counterparties, was it possible that risky trading activities could migrate from banks to nonfinancial firms if the exemption for hedging commercial risk were not in some way circumscribed?

Two versions of the MSP definition were considered in the Senate. The Banking Committee approved S. 3217 on April 15, 2010, including an MSP definition without the references to systemic importance that appeared in the House bill.[41] In other words, the regulators were given wide discretion to designate as MSPs firms that were not systemically important. The Senate Agriculture Committee produced another MSP definition, which was included in the bill that passed the Senate. It included "systemically significant" language generally similar to the House's, but added new prongs to the definition: an MSP would be any financial institution with a substantial position in any major swap category, or any financial entity that was highly

---

[41] Section 711 of S. 3217, as reported by the Senate Committee on Banking, Housing, and Urban Affairs, April 15, 2010.

leveraged.[42] This approach (together with changes to the clearing exemption limiting the exemption to nonfinancial entities) appeared likely to capture many swaps between dealers and other financial institutions, which make up more than half of the swap market.

Eliminating the clearing exemption for financial entities and bringing more financial firms under the MSP definition, as the Senate-passed bill did, had the potential to bring nearly all of the swaps trading under the new regulatory regime—the 38% of trades between dealers and the 44% between dealers and other financial institutions.[43] This approach did raise questions of equity, that is, should a small community bank or credit union be subject to more stringent regulation than a giant nonfinancial corporation with a much greater volume of swaps outstanding?

The final version of the legislation made several changes to the MSP definition and the clearing requirement. The "highly leveraged" prong of the MSP definition was amended to clarify that it did not apply to regulated depository institutions, which are normally highly leveraged. In addition, as noted above, regulators were given discretion to exempt certain financial institutions with less than $10 billion in assets from the mandatory clearing requirement. The precise number of firms that named MSPs (and the proportion of swaps that would ultimately be cleared) would depend on the SEC and CFTC rulemakings required by the act.

On May 23, 2012, the CFTC and SEC released a joint final rule further defining the terms "swap dealer" and "major swap participant."[44] The final rule defines what constitutes a "substantial" position in swaps, for the purposes of being an MSP. The regulators propose a two-pronged test for a "substantial" position. "Current exposure," or the current mark-to-market value of a swaps or security-based swaps position, minus the value of collateral posted against the position, constitutes a "substantial position" if the net uncollateralized exposure exceeds $1 billion, or $3 billion for interest rate or currency swaps. The second test also involves a calculation, this time relating to future exposure. This is calculated by discounting current notional exposure by a risk factor, by the existence of netting agreements, and according to whether the position is cleared or subject to daily margining. A future exposure is "substantial" if it exceeds $2 billion, or $6 billion for interest or currency rate swaps. These quantitative tests for "substantial position" are meant to set a threshold "materially below" the level at which a swaps trader's default could pose a threat to the financial system.

In the joint final rule, the CFTC's and SEC's definition of a swap dealer closely follows the Dodd-Frank definition of a swap dealer.[45] The final rule defines a "swap dealer" as any person (a person, in this case, can be an entity) who holds himself out as a dealer in swaps; makes a market in swaps; regularly enters into swaps with counterparties as an ordinary course of business for his own account; or engages in activity causing himself to be commonly known as a dealer or market maker in swaps. The rule also excludes certain swaps used to hedge or mitigate risk, if the risks

---

[42] This was not a "net" position, and applied to individual categories of swaps, as opposed to the institution's aggregate swaps book.

[43] The 38% and 44% figures are based on BIS data released in May 2010 for total global notional amounts outstanding as of December, 2009. Since much of the drafting of the bills that ultimately became the Dodd-Frank Act occurred prior to May, 2010, prior figures using earlier data may have looked slightly different. The May 2010 BIS data is available at http://www.bis.org/statistics/otcder/dt1920a.pdf.

[44] Commodity Futures Trading Commission and the Securities and Exchange Commission, "Further Definition of 'Swap Dealer,'" "Major Swap Participant," and "Eligible Contract Participant." 77 *Federal Register* 30596, May 23, 2012. Available at http://www.cftc.gov/ucm/groups/public/@lrfederalregister/documents/file/2012-10562a.pdf.

[45] Section 721 of the Dodd-Frank Act.

arise from a potential change in the value of assets a person owns or produces, or services the person provides. It also excludes swaps entered into between majority-owned affiliates. At the same time, the rule includes a de minimus exception. In order for a person to be regarded as a swap dealer, the aggregate gross notional amount of the swaps the person entered into during the prior 12 months in connection with swap dealing activities must exceed $8 billion during a phase-in period. The phase-in period would last two and a half years from the time data starts being reported to swap data repositories. After this time, the CFTC will undertake a study of the swap markets, and may reduce this de minimus amount to $3 billion, or may propose a new rule for a different de minimus threshold.

Reporting of Swaps and Security-Based Swaps

Swaps must be reported to registered swap data repositories or the CFTC.[46] Security-based swaps must be reported to registered security-based swap data repositories or to the SEC.[47] The Dodd-Frank Act requires all swaps to be reported.[48] Swaps and security-based swaps entered into prior to the date of the enactment of Dodd-Frank Act are exempt from the clearing requirement if they are reported in accordance with the act. Swaps and security-based swaps entered into after the enactment of the Dodd-Frank Act, but prior to the imposition of the clearing requirement, are exempt from the clearing requirement if they are reported in accordance with the act.

Section 727 of Dodd-Frank outlines the public availability of swap transaction data.[49] The CFTC is required to promulgate rules regarding the public availability of such data. Swaps that are subject to the clearing requirement, and swaps that are not subject to the clearing requirement, but are nonetheless cleared at registered derivatives clearing organizations, must have real-time reporting for such transactions. Real-time reporting means to report data relating to a swap transaction, including price and volume, as soon as technologically practicable after the time at which the swap transaction has been executed. For swaps that are not cleared and are reported pursuant to subsection (h)(6) (requiring reporting prior to the implementation of the clearing requirement), real-time reporting is required in a manner that does not disclose the business transactions and market positions of any person. Lastly, for swaps that are determined to be required to be cleared under subsection (h)(2) (outlining the two ways, discussed above, in which swaps may become subject to the clearing requirement), but are not cleared, real-time public reporting is required as well. There is no parallel requirement in the act for security-based swaps, presumably because national securities exchanges upon which these transactions will be executed already provide comparable reporting.[50]

The act also creates reporting obligations for uncleared swaps and security-based swaps (including swaps and security-based swaps that qualify for the end-user exemption).[51] Swaps entered into prior to the enactment of the act will be subject to reporting and recordkeeping

---

[46] Section 723(a)(3) of the Dodd-Frank Act (to be codified at 7 U.S.C. §2(h)(5)).

[47] Section 763(a) of the Dodd-Frank Act (to be codified at 15 U.S.C. § 78a *et seq.*).

[48] Sections 3103 and 3203 of H.R. 4173 (as passed); Sections 723(a) and 763 of S. 3217 (as passed).

[49] Section 725 of the Dodd-Frank Act (to be codified at 7 U.S.C. §2(a)).

[50] *See* 15 U.S.C. § 78f.

[51] Section 729 of the Dodd-Frank Act (to be codified at 7 U.S.C. §6o-1) and Section 766 of the Dodd-Frank Act (to be codified at 15 U.S.C. §78a *et seq.*).

requirements for uncleared swaps and security-based swaps.[52] The purpose of these requirements, presumably, is to give the relevant commissions access to a more complete picture of the derivatives market, even for swaps that are not required to be cleared.

The SEC proposed its rule on reporting requirements for security-based swaps, which was published on December 2, 2010.[53] Regulation SBSR (for "security-based swap reporting") would require security-based swap data repositories to register with the SEC as securities information processors, an existing category of regulated entity. The data that the repositories receive will fall into two categories: one to be made public and the other non-public. Information to be disclosed to the public will include

- information on the asset class and the underlying security;
- the price and notional amount of the security-based swap;
- the time of execution; and
- the effective and expiration dates of the security-based swap.

Non-public information—to be available to the SEC—includes

- the identity of the swap counterparty, the broker, and the trading desk;
- any up-front payments;
- the title of the master agreement (if any);
- a description of the valuation methods to be used; and
- which counterparty will report the contract to the data repository.

Some market participants expressed concerns that "real-time" reporting (required by the statute, but left to the regulators to define) would be unduly burdensome for large or illiquid trades, where reporting might result in the disclosure of market-sensitive information about holders of large positions and their trading intentions. The SEC, however, proposed a narrow definition of "real-time"—"as soon as technologically practicable after the time at which the ... transaction has been executed."[54]

There are only a few circumstances where the real-time reporting requirement is qualified. In the case of contracts that are not required to be cleared and are not cleared, public reporting for such transactions shall not disclose the business transactions and market positions of any person. In addition, the SEC proposal does not address block trades directly, but notes that the SEC intends to propose a rule for reporting of block trades at a later date, after considering comments.[55]

---

[52] *Id.*

[53] SEC, "Regulation SBSR – Reporting and Dissemination of Security-Based Swap Information," (Release No. 34-63346; File No. S7-34-10), *Federal Register,* v. 75, December 2, 2010, p. 75208.

[54] Ibid., p. 75210.

[55] Block trades are very large securities transactions, which would be expected to move prices if they were executed on a public exchange. Securities markets have developed a number of mechanisms to match large buyers and sellers without revealing the size of the deal to the public markets, which would raise the cost of the transaction to the block traders. These include the upstairs market and dark pools, where block trades can be negotiated out of the public eye.

On April 3, 2012, the CFTC issued a final rule describing reporting, recordkeeping and daily trading records obligations for swap dealers and MSPs.[56] The CFTC's final rule followed a proposed rule released on December 23, 2010.[57] The CFTC's final rule calls for electronic reporting to a swap data repository (SDR) of swap data from each of two important stages of the existence of a swap: the creation of the swap, and the continuation of the swap over its existence until its final termination or expiration. The purpose of this appears to be to create an electronic audit trail of all stages of the swap.[58] The final rule requires swap dealers and MSPs to maintain records of all activities related to the business of the swap dealers or MSPs, regardless of whether they also have a prudential, or banking, regulator, with separate recordkeeping requirements.

Prevention of Evasion

The CFTC and SEC have the authority under the Dodd-Frank Act to promulgate rules the commissions determine to be necessary to "prevent evasions of the mandatory clearing requirements under this Act." However, this rulemaking authority, while broad, carries additional nuance described below.

As noted above, the statutory scheme of Dodd-Frank creates two ways in which a swap or security-based swap may become subject to the clearing requirement. In one scenario, derivatives clearing organizations and clearing agencies submit the swaps and security-based swaps they intend to clear to the CFTC or SEC and the agency determines whether to apply the clearing requirement to the transactions. In the other scenario, the CFTC and SEC are required to engage in an ongoing independent review of swaps and security-based swaps under their jurisdiction to determine whether those transactions should be subject to the mandatory clearing requirement. It is thus possible that the CFTC and SEC could identify swaps and security-based swaps that "would otherwise be subject to the clearing requirement" but for the fact that no derivatives clearing organization or clearing agency accepts them for clearing.

In that event, the relevant agency (CFTC for swaps, and SEC for security-based swaps) is required to investigate the relevant facts and circumstances, issue a public report of its investigation, and "take such actions as the Commission determines to be necessary and in the public interest, which may include requiring the retaining of adequate margin or capital by parties to the swap [or security-based swap], group, category, type, or class of swaps [or security-based swaps]."[59] However, neither the CFTC nor the SEC may "adopt rules requiring a derivatives clearing organization [or clearing agency] to list for clearing a swap, group, category, type, or class of swaps if the clearing of the swap, group, category, type, or class of swaps would threaten the financial integrity of the derivatives organization."[60]

---

[56] Commodity Futures Trading Commission, "Swap Dealer and Major Swap Participant Recordkeeping, Reporting and Duties Rules," 77 *Federal Register* 20128, April 3, 2012. Available at http://www.cftc.gov/ucm/groups/public/@lrfederalregister/documents/file/2012-5317a.pdf.

[57] CFTC, "17 CFR Part 49: Swap Data Repositories," *Federal Register*, v. 75, December 23, 2010, p. 80897.

[58] See Commodity Futures Trading Commission, "Swap Dealer and Major Swap Participant Recordkeeping, Reporting and Duties Rules," 77 *Federal Register* 20128, April 3, 2012 at p. 20212: "Appendix 2: Statement of Chairman Gary Gensler."

[59] Section 723(a)(3) of the Dodd-Frank Act (codified at 7 U.S.C. §2(h)(4)) (swaps); Section 763(a) of the Dodd-Frank Act (codified at 15 U.S.C. § 78a *et seq.*)(security-based swaps).

[60] Section 723(a)(3) of the Dodd-Frank Act (codified at 7 U.S.C. §2(h)(4)) (swaps); Section 763(a) of the Dodd-Frank Act (codified at 15 U.S.C. § 78a *et seq.*)(security-based swaps).

Because the clearing requirement has not yet been fully implemented, it does not appear that the CFTC has exercised rulemaking authority pursuant to these provisions. However, in its rule proposal for implementing Dodd-Frank's clearing requirement, the CFTC also includes a proposal of rules for the prevention of evasion of the clearing requirement.[61] A final rule has not yet been issued.

The SEC, however, has issued its rules implementing Dodd-Frank's clearing requirement, and among those rules were certain provisions intended to prevent evasion of the clearing requirement.[62] For example, the SEC recognized that some entities may provide different clearing functions, but that those functions were not always the equivalent of "central clearing" of security-based swaps by a central counterparty (CCP). As a result, the SEC has issued a rule that requires market participants to submit security-based swaps to clearing agencies that function as CCPs.

Enhanced CFTC Authority over Commodities Markets

In 2008, as energy and grain prices set new records, speculators in derivatives were blamed by some for price volatility and for price levels that many observers believed were not justified by the underlying economic fundamentals. Although the CFTC maintained that markets were functioning normally and that the price discovery process was not being distorted, the 110th Congress considered legislation intended to insulate commodity prices from the impact of excessive speculation and manipulation. Congress implemented this goal by including a number of provisions in Title VII of the Dodd-Frank Act that enhanced the authority of the CFTC to police these markets and impose limits where the agency saw a need. To this end, Congress enhanced the CFTC's power to set margin and position limits and also amended the CFTC's authority to prohibit manipulation in markets for commodities and swaps. What follows is a brief description of the current status of these enhanced authorities.

Margin Requirements

Section 736 of the Dodd-Frank Act granted the CFTC the authority to set margin requirements for futures exchanges, as the CFTC finds to be necessary and appropriate for the protection of persons producing, handling, processing, or consuming any commodity traded for future delivery, or for the protection of traders or to insure fair dealing in commodities traded for future delivery.[63] The CFTC may set margin at certain registered entities under the condition that the rule or order issued by the agency be limited to protecting the financial integrity of a DCO, be designed for risk management purposes to protect financial integrity of transactions, and not set

---

[61] 77 Fed. Reg. 47170 (August 7, 2012) available at http://www.cftc.gov/ucm/groups/public/@lrfederalregister/ documents/file/2012-18382a.pdf.

[62] SEC, Process for Submissions for Review of Security-Based Swaps for Mandatory Clearing and Notice Filing Requirements for Clearing Agencies; Technical Amendments to Rule 19b-4 and Form 19b-4 Applicable to All Self Regulatory Organizations, Final Rule, Release No. 34-67286 (June 28, 2012) available at http://www.sec.gov/rules/ final/2012/34-67286.pdf.

[63] Codified at 7 U.S.C. §12a(7).

specific margin amounts. It does not appear that the CFTC has had occasion to use this authority since the passage of the act.

Position Limits

Section 737 of the Dodd-Frank Act appeared to direct the CFTC to establish position limits for swaps and futures. The law says that "the Commission shall by rule, regulation, or order establish limits on the amount of positions, as appropriate, other than bona fide hedge positions, that may be held by any person."[64] Believing this language required the CFTC to set position limits, regardless of whether position limits were determined to be necessary or appropriate to curb speculation in a given market, the CFTC approved rules setting position limits for certain commodities in November of 2011.[65] Industry groups challenged the regulations in court, arguing that Section 737 amended a broader statute, and, when analyzed in the proper statutory context, the CFTC was only required to set position limit rules where the Commission had found the rules to be necessary and appropriate for the market upon which the rules were imposed. The opponents of the position limit rules argued the rules issued by the CFTC violated the Commodity Exchange Act because the CFTC had not conducted the appropriate analysis to determine whether the rules were necessary and appropriate prior to issuing the rules.

The U.S. District Court for the District of Columbia vacated and remanded the CFTC's position limit rules in a decision issued in September of 2012.[66] Courts usually defer to the interpretation of the agency charged with implementing a statute, but only if the agency has reasonably interpreted an ambiguity that the agency acknowledges exists in the statute.[67] Here, the court could not give deference to the CFTC's interpretation of the statute, because the agency had erroneously found the statute to be unambiguous.[68] As a result of the court's decision to vacate the rules, the agency must now determine whether position limits are required by the act regardless of whether the limits are found by the agency to be necessary, prior to promulgating new rules.

Anti-Manipulation Authority

Section 753 also amended the Commodity Exchange Act (CEA) to broaden the CFTC's anti-manipulation authority and add new prohibitions against false reporting and providing misleading information to the CFTC.[69] Following the enactment of Dodd-Frank, Section 6(c)(1) of the CEA now provides that

> It shall be unlawful for any person directly or indirectly to use or employ or attempt to use or employ, in connection with any swap or a contract of sale of any commodity in interstate commerce, or for future delivery on or subject to the rules of any registered entity, any

---

[64] Codified at 7 U.S.C. §6a(a).

[65] 76 Fed. Reg. 7126 (November 18, 2011) available at http://www.cftc.gov/ucm/groups/public/@lrfederalregister/documents/file/2011-28809a.pdf.

[66] International Swaps and Derivatives Association v. CFTC, Civil Action No. 11-cv-2146 (RLW), 2012 U.S. Dist. LEXIS 139788 (U.S.D.C. September 28, 2012).

[67] Peter Pan Bus Lines v. Feds Motor Carrier Safety Administration, 471 F.2d 1350 (D.C. Cir. 2006).

[68] International Swaps and Derivatives Association v. CFTC, Civil Action No. 11-cv-2146 (RLW), 2012 U.S. Dist. LEXIS 139788 (U.S.D.C. September 28, 2012).

[69] Section 729 of the Dodd-Frank Act (codified at 7 U.S.C. §9).

manipulative or deceptive device or contrivance, in contravention of such rules and regulations as the Commission shall promulgate ... [70]

The CFTC has issued regulations implementing this authority.[71] In its order adopting the new regulations, the CFTC likened the language in this section to Section 10b of the Securities Exchange Act of 1934 and to the Securities and Exchange Commission's rule 10b-5, implementing Section 10b. Section 10b, according to the Supreme Court, was designed as a "catchall clause to prevent fraudulent practices."[72] The CFTC determined that the language of CEA Section 6(c)(1) was designed to operate similarly as a catchall to prevent fraudulent practices in violation of the CEA.[73] The CFTC found, therefore, that, to the extent possible, the CFTC would interpret violations of Section 6(c)(1) similarly to violations of Section 10b and would base its analysis on the well-established body of law developed pursuant to Section 10b and Rule 10b-5. As a result, the CFTC decided to implement its new anti-manipulation authority flexibly, in keeping with the remedial purpose of the act. This case-by-case approach, rather than setting detailed rules, is also similar to the SEC's approach to prosecuting securities fraud.

The CFTC has had occasion to use this new authority to obtain settlements with market participants. In data released on October 5, 2012, the CFTC revealed that it had, among other enforcement actions, imposed the largest fine for violations of the anti-manipulation provisions of the CEA in CFTC history in 2012.[74] In that case, Barclays Bank, PLC had admitted to both United Kingdom and United States regulators that the bank had submitted false reports of its borrowing rates to the British Bankers Association (BBA) for the U.S. London Interbank Offered Rate ("LIBOR"), an index that purports to measure the interest rates at which banks may borrow funds from each other. Barclays admitted, at times, to submitting knowingly false rates at the request of some of the bank's derivative traders, when the traders believed that a higher or lower LIBOR would improve their position on certain investments. Barclays also admitted that during the financial crisis it began to suspect that other member banks that were submitting rates to the BBA were understating their borrowing costs. In order to manage public perception of the bank and to prevent investors from questioning the health of the bank, Barclay's began to report borrowing costs to the BBA that were below the bank's actual borrowing costs. The CFTC found, based upon its investigation into the matter, that Barclays was likely guilty of violating Section 6(c)(1) of the CEA.[75] In its agreement with the CFTC, Barclays did not admit to violating the CEA, but has agreed to pay a $200 million fine and to comply with certain internal controls designed to prevent future LIBOR manipulation stipulated by the CFTC in its order. With the broader authority to prevent and prosecute fraudulent activity provided to the CFTC in the Dodd-Frank Act, enforcement actions similar to the Barclay's fine are expected in the future.[76]

---

[70] codified at 7 U.S.C. §9.

[71] 76 Fed. Reg. 41398 (July 14, 2011).

[72] Chiarella v. U.S. 445 U.S. 222, 226 (1980).

[73] 76 Fed. Reg. 41398 (July 14, 2011).

[74] CFTC, CFTC Releases Enforcement Division's Annual Results, October 5, 2012, available at http://www.cftc.gov/PressRoom/PressReleases/pr6378-12.

[75] In the Matter of Barclay's, PLC Order Instituting Proceedings Pursuant to Section 6(c) and 6(d) of the Commodity Exchange Act, As Amended, Making Findings, and Imposing Remedial Sanctions, CFTC Docket No. 12-25 (June 27, 2012) available at http://www.cftc.gov/ucm/groups/public/@lrenforcementactions/documents/legalpleading/enfbarclaysorder062712.pdf.

[76] Peter J. Henning, CFTC is Set to Get Tougher on Fraud, NYTimes Blog, (November 1, 2010) available at http://dealbook.nytimes.com/2010/11/01/c-f-t-c-is-set-to-get-tougher-on-fraud/.

Section 716—Prohibition on Federal Assistance to Swaps Entities

Section 716 originated in the Senate Agriculture Committee and was included in the bill that passed the Senate in May 2010. The section prohibited federal assistance, defined as the use of any funds to loan money to, buy the securities or other assets of, or to enter into "any assistance arrangement" with a "swaps entity." Swaps entities included swap dealers and major swap participants (and the equivalents in security-based swaps), securities and futures exchanges, SEFs, and clearing organizations registered with the CFTC, the SEC, or any other federal or state agency.

The intent of the provision was to ensure that taxpayer funds would not have to be used to meet obligations of financial institutions engaged in risky derivatives trading. Such activity was deemed too risky to be under the federal safety net that covers insured depository institutions. The Chairwoman of the Senate Agriculture Committee at the time, Senator Lincoln explained it this way:

> This provision seeks to ensure that banks get back to the business of banking. Under our current system, there are a handful of big banks that are simply no longer acting like banks.... In my view, banks were never intended to perform these [derivatives] activities, which have been the single largest factor to these institutions growing so large that taxpayers had no choice but to bail them out in order to prevent total economic ruin.[77]

Supporters of the original version of Section 716 described it as an appropriate means to compel banks to spin off their swap dealings, or to "push them out" into separately capitalized affiliates. Opponents of the measure argued that the definitions of federal assistance and swaps entity were so broadly drafted that there might be unanticipated consequences. For example, if Citigroup sold off its swap dealer operations, it would still have hundreds of billions of loans and other risky assets on its balance sheet, which it would need to hedge with interest rate swaps and other derivatives. This hedging activity would likely put the bank into the major swap participant category, and thus foreclose access to the discount window, FDIC insurance, and other features of the safety net. Similarly, if the Federal Reserve were supplying liquidity to the financial system during a future crisis, would it be prudent to deny such support to clearinghouses which represent concentrations of risk?

The conference committee adopted a modified version of Section 716, which narrowed the definitions of swaps entity and permitted banks to act as swap dealers under some circumstances. In the final legislation, exchanges, SEFs, and clearing organizations are not swaps entities. In addition, the term "swaps entity" does not include a major swap participant or major security-based swap participant that is an insured depository institution.

The final version clarifies that the prohibition on aid does not prevent a bank from creating an affiliate that is a swaps entity, provided that the affiliate complies with sections 23A and 23B of the Federal Reserve Act and other requirements of the Fed, the SEC, and the CFTC. Moreover, the bank itself may continue to act as a swaps dealer for contracts involving rates or reference assets that are permissible for investment by a national bank. This means that banks can continue

---

[77] Remarks of Senator Blanche Lincoln, *Congressional Record*, May 5, 2010, p. S3140.

as dealers in swaps linked to interest rates, currencies, government securities, and precious metals, but not other commodities or equities. Credit default swaps are treated as a special category: banks may deal in them if they are cleared by a derivatives clearing organization regulated by the SEC or CFTC. Dealing in uncleared credit default swaps, however, is not deemed to be a permissible bank activity.

Finally, Section 716 mandates that no taxpayer funds may be used to prevent the liquidation of a swaps entity. Any funds expended in such a liquidation proceeding, and not covered by the swaps entity's assets, may be recouped through assessments on the financial sector.

Section 716 has not taken effect yet. A guidance issued by the Office of the Comptroller of the Currency, the Board of Governors of the Federal Reserve, and the Federal Deposit Insurance Corporation has indicated that Section 716 will not take effect until July 16, 2013.[78]

Author Contact Information

Rena S. Miller
Analyst in Financial Economics
rsmiller@crs.loc.gov, 7-0826

Kathleen Ann Ruane
Legislative Attorney
kruane@crs.loc.gov, 7-9135

Acknowledgments

Parts of the introductory material in this report are adapted from CRS Report R40965, *Key Issues in Derivatives Reform,* by Rena S. Miller.

---

[78] 77 Fed. Reg. 27456 (May 10, 2012), available at http://www.gpo.gov/fdsys/pkg/FR-2012-05-10/pdf/2012-11326.pdf.